D0773641

MANDY MOORE

A Real-Life Reader Biography

John Bankston

Mitchell Lane Publishers, Inc.
P.O. Box 619
Bear, Delaware 19701

First Printing

Real-Life Reader Biographies

Paula Abdul	Mary Joe Fernandez	Ricky Martin	Arnold Schwarzenegger
Christina Aguilera	Andres Galarraga	Mark McGwire	Selena
Marc Anthony	Sarah Michelle Gellar	Alyssa Milano	Maurice Sendak
Drew Barrymore	Jeff Gordon	**Mandy Moore**	Dr. Seuss
Brandy	Mia Hamm	Chuck Norris	Shakira
Garth Brooks	Melissa Joan Hart	Tommy Nuñez	Alicia Silverstone
Kobe Bryant	Jennifer Love Hewitt	Rosie O'Donnell	Jessica Simpson
Sandra Bullock	Faith Hill	Rafael Palmeiro	Sinbad
Mariah Carey	Hollywood Hogan	Gary Paulsen	Jimmy Smits
Cesar Chavez	Katie Holmes	Freddie Prinze, Jr.	Sammy Sosa
Christopher Paul Curtis	Enrique Iglesias	Julia Roberts	Britney Spears
Roald Dahl	Derek Jeter	Robert Rodriguez	Sheryl Swoopes
Oscar De La Hoya	Steve Jobs	J.K. Rowling	Shania Twain
Trent Dimas	Michelle Kwan	Keri Russell	Liv Tyler
Celine Dion	Bruce Lee	Winona Ryder	Robin Williams
Sheila E.	Jennifer Lopez	Cristina Saralegui	Vanessa Williams
Gloria Estefan	Cheech Marin		Tiger Woods

Library of Congress Cataloging-in-Publication Data
Bankston, John, 1974-
    Mandy Moore/John Bankston.
        p. cm.—(A Real-life reader biography)
    Includes index.
    ISBN 1-58415-073-4
    1. Moore, Mandy, 1984—Juvenile literature. Singers—United States—Biography—Juvenile literature. [1. Moore, Mandy, 1984- 2. Singers. 3. Actors and actresses.] I. Title. II. Series.
ML3930.M68 B36 2001
782.4216'092—dc21
[B]   2001029455

ABOUT THE AUTHOR: Born in Boston, Massachussetts, John Bankston began publishing articles in newspapers and magazines while still a teenager. Since then, he has written over two hundred articles, and contributed chapters to books such as *Crimes of Passion*, and *Death Row 2000*, which have been sold in bookstores across the world. He currently lives in Los Angeles, California, pursuing a career in the entertainment industry. He has worked as a writer for the movie *Dot-Com*, which began filming in winter 2000, and is finishing his first young adult novel.

PHOTO CREDITS: cover: Shooting Star; p. 4 Laurie Steiner; p. 7 Shooting Star; p. 11 Globe Photos; p. 12 Shooting Star; p. 17 Scott Harrison/Archive Photos; p. 23 Paul Fenton/Shooting Star; p. 26 Globe Photos; p. 28 Corbis; p. 30 Globe Photos

ACKNOWLEDGMENTS: The following story has been thoroughly researched, and to the best of our knowledge, represents a true story. While every possible effort has been made to ensure accuracy, the publisher will not assume liability for damages caused by inaccuracies in the data, and makes no warranty on the accuracy of the information contained herein. This story has not been authorized nor endorsed by Mandy Moore.

Table of Contents

Chapter 1
National Anthem Girl

The most unlikely person can change your life forever. For singer Mandy Moore, that person was an overnight delivery man. Because he was impressed by her talent and ability, he helped put her on the road to superstardom.

Before the day he saw Mandy Moore sing, it had been a long road until she was at the right place, at the right time.

Amanda Leigh "Mandy" Moore was born on April 10, 1984 in Nashua, New Hampshire. The mainly rural New England state is known for green, pine-covered mountains, cool clean lakes and

Amanda Leigh Moore was born in Nashua, New Hampshire.

a tiny coastline. But although it's beautiful, New Hampshire probably isn't the best place to break into the music business.

In the 1980s, many well-known rock stars were discovered performing in Los Angeles, California. In the early 1990s, Seattle, Washington was the place to be for those seeking fame in the music business. By the late 1990s, Orlando, Florida became the destination for those who wanted pop music stardom.

For decades Orlando was mainly known for its theme parks. Millions of people traveled from around the world to visit places like Disney World, Universal Studios and Epcot Center. To these tourists, Orlando's most famous resident was Mickey Mouse.

Today, the city is more than just theme parks and Mickey. It is also where many entertainers get their starts. Television stars like Melissa Joan Hart from "Sabrina, The Teenage Witch" and "Felicity's" Keri Russell got their first

Mandy and her family moved to Orlando, Florida when she was just a baby.

Mandy enjoys all the fame and stardom she has received. Disney sponsors many of her events. Growing up in Florida has made it easier for her to have a music career.

big break performing on television programs produced in Orlando.

Singers Britney Spears and Christina Aguilera, along with 'N Sync and The Backstreet Boys, also got their start there.

So even though Mandy's parents—airline pilot Don, and mother Stacy, a former reporter—didn't have any idea that their daughter would become a famous singer, they picked one of the best places for her to launch her career by moving to Orlando when she was only six months old. In many ways, they were just like any other family hoping to trade the frigid Northeastern winters for warm Orlando sunshine.

Except Mandy Moore wasn't like any other little girl.

At the age of six, she realized exactly what she wanted to do with her life. While attending Park Maitland School, she saw a performance of the musical "Oklahoma." Sitting in the audience, she knew she wanted to be a singer.

At the age of six, Mandy knew she wanted to be a singer.

She went home and told her parents about her dream.

They weren't convinced. They thought six was too young. They didn't think she was ready.

But Mandy was persistent. She constantly sang a lot of different songs while she was around the house. Finally her parents gave in and let her get voice lessons. She also attended a summer musical theatre camp.

Soon she started to appear in local productions of famous musicals such as "Guys and Dolls" and "The Sound of Music."

And not long after that, all her hard work began to pay off.

When she was nine years old, she performed before her largest audience. They weren't there to see a play. They were there to watch an Orlando Magic professional basketball game.

Mandy Moore stood alone at center court in front of a crowd of well over 10,000 people who were waiting for the game to start. There was a hush as she

Her parents let her have voice lessons and sent her to a summer musical theatre camp.

began to sing a song which has challenged performers much older and far more experienced than she was.

She sang the National Anthem.

She sang it so well that other local teams and sporting events like the Chris Evert Pro-Celebrity Tennis Tournament asked Mandy to sing the National Anthem for them. She got her very first taste of fame.

In Orlando, Mandy Moore became known as "The National Anthem Girl."

Soon she began working on television, shooting pilots—or tryout shows—for Disney and Nickelodeon, both of which had studios in Orlando. Because she was well-spoken and poised, she also did voice-overs. Voice-overs are where performers' voices are used, but they aren't seen. Cartoons are an example of where voice-overs are used. Kids who can speak clearly are very much in demand for this type of work.

And Mandy began doing commercials. It was during the filming of a commercial that she was spotted by the overnight delivery driver. He couldn't believe such a young girl had such a great singing voice. During a break, he approached her and her mother. He convinced them to give him a demo tape—a recording of Mandy singing.

Although the driver wasn't in the music business, he had a friend who was. Dave McPherson worked in Sony's Artists and Repertoire. This is the department in charge of finding new talent. Mandy and her mother figured they didn't have anything to lose, so they gave the tape to the driver.

Around Orlando, Mandy became known as "The National Anthem Girl." She was asked to sing the National Anthem before many pro games.

He quickly gave it to his friend, who brought it to an executive at Epic/550 Records. Everyone who listened to the tape knew this girl was special.

They called Mandy Moore and got her to audition. She sang for them, and that very same weekend, they signed her to a recording contract.

Because a delivery driver believed in her, Mandy Moore got her first record deal.

She was fourteen years old.

Chapter 2
"Candy"

Some singers blaze trails. They are the first ones to perform in certain ways or to popularize a style of music. From Elvis in the 1950s and Jimi Hendrix in the 1960s to Kurt Cobain in the 1990s, performers who broke through and became famous led the way for many similar acts to follow.

In some ways, performers who come after established acts have a more difficult time. Sure, there are people to emulate, or copy. The problem is that listeners often make comparisons to the original.

Mandy got her first record deal when she was 14 years old.

Mandy understood that she was part of a music trend. She was a blonde pop star.

Sometimes this makes it impossible for the singers who follow to step out from the original's shadow. Of course this didn't keep 'N Sync from becoming as popular as the Backstreet Boys.

Mandy Moore understood that she was part of a current music trend. She was a blonde pop singer. She knew she'd be compared to singers like Britney Spears, Christina Aguilera and Jessica Simpson.

But comparisons like that didn't bother Mandy. Deep down, she believed that she was different from the others. All they had in common, she thought, was blonde hair and pop music.

Mandy Moore spent the early part of 1999 recording her first album, which was called "So Real." Producers from Jive Records who had been involved with the Backstreet Boys, 'N Sync and Britney Spears worked on the CD.

Although the songs for "So Real" were written by other people, Mandy Moore was able to draw on her own experiences when she sang them. For example, when she recorded "Candy," she thought about an old boyfriend. She liked him—sort of—but she was also still mad at him. So that added a little "grit" to the way she recorded it.

It is that "grit"—a bluesy, throaty delivery—that would be even more apparent when Mandy performed live. But before she could perform, Mandy's label Epic/550 knew they had to do one thing. They had to build an audience for Mandy's singing.

Just a few years ago, building an audience took years. Singers had to perform at smaller clubs and go on tour to make a name for themselves before an album could be released.

But these days, the Internet has changed everything. In March of 1999, Epic set up two Mandy Moore websites. One was designed by the same company that had already designed successful websites for The Backstreet Boys and 'N Sync. By setting up these websites, the record label attracted more listeners in a very short time than if

In 1999, Mandy recorded her first album, "So Real."

Mandy had been performing in clubs for years. Currently the two sites receive over 100,000 hits per day.

In the summer of 1999, Mandy began touring as an opening act for the Backstreet Boys and 'N Sync. Although her CD hadn't been released yet, Mandy already had fans. Lots of fans. Many of them waited in line for more than two hours to meet her and get her autograph.

Mandy was amazed. "It's a cool feeling for somebody to want your name scribbled on a piece of paper," she said. "I never want to get used to that feeling."

Although Mandy's fans lined up to meet her, the singer's career didn't take off as quickly as Britney Spears' or Christina Aguilera's. When it was released, Aguilera's first CD was on *Billboard* Magazine's Top Ten list. When Mandy Moore's album "So Real" came out in the fall of 1999, it entered the Billboard charts as number 77. However, no one considered this a failure.

Mandy's goal wasn't to be an overnight star, it was to have a long, developing career. Later in 1999 "Candy" became one of the most requested songs on pop radio and "So Real" eventually went platinum. This means it sold over one million copies.

And a hit CD was just the beginning.

Here is Mandy at the 1999 Billboard Music Awards at the MGM Grand hotel, Las Vegas, Nevada, December 8, 1999.

Chapter 3
"So Real"

Although she was still only in her mid-teens, Mandy Moore had enough experience working in commercials to know how a blonde female pop star might be seen. She thought that people might just think of her as a sort of product.

That's because the music business is just that—a business. Popular performers are advertised and promoted just like products such as cereal or soda. The problem is, when people are treated as products they are often "packaged." That means their entire look is designed for them by other

> Mandy didn't really want to be seen as a "packaged product."

people. Because of this, some performers are presented in ways which may be completely wrong for them.

Pop singers like Britney Spears and Christina Aguilera have been criticized for wearing clothes which are too revealing. Girls who are eight years old sometimes try to dress like their favorite singers, who are often ten years older.

Mandy Moore has said repeatedly that isn't what she wanted to have happen to her. She doesn't want to attract attention to herself just by wearing tight clothes. It may work for other people, but it's the wrong message for her.

One of the most important things to Mandy Moore was staying the same person she had been before she became a famous singer.

A few times people tried to make her fit a certain image. Her hair was "floofed up" and her eyes were darkened with makeup. That made her uncomfortable and less confident. She much prefers to look like she really is

She likes to stay "real." It is important to her that she stays the same person she was before she became a famous singer.

> **It's important to Mandy that she not be someone else's idea of what a pop star should be.**

because she's very comfortable with her looks.

As Mandy continued to tour in support of her first album, she realized how important it was to show others that she wasn't just a packaged product. She wasn't someone else's invention or idea of what a pop star was supposed to be.

She often says how lucky she is that she doesn't have people telling her how to dress and to act. She believes that it is very important to show people that she can be herself and that she isn't someone who just goes along with the crowd.

Mandy Moore doesn't just think it's important to stay the same. She feels it's important to let kids who look up to her know she isn't letting others try to change her.

She loves to talk with people and show them that no one is out there trying to invent a personality for her. It's especially important for her to prove that she's different because she's often being compared to other singers.

By late 1999, Mandy had her first opportunity to fight those comparisons. Her first CD, "So Real," was described by many people as "bubblegum pop." Bubblegum pop is a term used to describe music which is very sweet, like bubblegum, and doesn't have much substance to it.

Mandy began recording brand new songs—songs which were completely different from the ones on "So Real."

When her manager played those new songs for the record company, they were surprised. At first they didn't even recognize that it was Mandy who had recorded them.

New Songs like "I Wanna Be With You," "Everything My Heart Desires," and "Your Face" weren't like Britney Spears. If people were forced to compare them, they thought of mid-90s folk singer Jewel. All of the songs were more mature, and deeper.

Her first CD, "So Real," was described as "bubble–gum pop."

The record company loved the new songs. So they combined the new songs with a remix of "Candy" and songs from "So Real" to form a new CD. This Special Edition, entitled "I Wanna Be With You," was released on May 9, 2000.

Because it had been only a few months since her first album had come out, it was unusual to release another album so soon. Although "Candy," the hit single from "So Real" was still on the *Billboard* charts, releasing "I Wanna Be With You" made sense. It would prove Mandy wasn't just like all the other female blonde pop stars she was lumped in with.

The new CD would also attract a wider audience—not just kids her own age but older people as well.

For example, at a radio station in Charleston, South Carolina, the promotions director brought the new CD to a music meeting but didn't tell anyone who the artist was. Most of the people listening were women in their twenties who liked rock music. They all

"I Wanna Be With You" was her next hit.

liked what they heard. Then the promotions director told them that it was Mandy's music. At first they were embarrassed that they actually liked something by Mandy Moore, but then they realized how much she had advanced.

Mandy Moore had definitely set herself apart from other pop stars. Her next step was to prove she was more than just a singer.

Mandy at the Teen Choice Awards, August 8, 2000.

Chapter 4
Not Just a Pop Star

Many young girls see Mandy as a role model.

Everyone needs role models. By looking at someone who has succeeded in a way you'd like to, it's possible to get an idea of what steps you might need to take. For example, if you want to be successful in science, perhaps the careers of Jonas Salk or Albert Einstein can provide some guidance for you. Someone who is interested in making movies might want to take a look at Steven Spielberg's career as a movie director.

In 1999 many young singers might have seen Mandy Moore as a role model. She was fifteen, her CD was popular, and she was standing up for herself in a career where many young performers let other people make all the important decisions.

Despite all of her obvious fame and success, Mandy Moore still drew inspiration from other performers. Although she admired the work of other successful teen recording stars, Mandy had different role models.

Mandy has said that Madonna and Bette Midler are her two biggest influences. She likes them because they are more than just singers. They are all-around performers who make records, act in TV shows and movies, and appear on stage.

One of the first steps that Mandy Moore made to branch out from her career as a singer was to become a spokeswoman for Neutrogena skin care products. She believes their products are clean and fresh—which is exactly how many people describe her. Many people see her on television promoting Neutrogena.

Mandy wants her career to be more than just a teen recording star.

Mandy sings for the crowd at a CD signing to promote her new song, "I Wanna Be With You."

Of course, working in commercials wasn't new for Mandy. She had already done that when she was starting her career in Orlando.

The popularity of her music video for the song "Candy" gave Mandy another opportunity to move beyond singing. As the song became a regular pick on MTV's viewer vote in the program "Total Request Live," she made frequent appearances. She seemed comfortable on the show, answering questions from the audience and talking about her life.

Because Mandy Moore was so at ease in front of a

camera, she was given her own program "Mandy." At fifteen she became one of the youngest hosts in MTV history. Since she tapes the entire week's worth of episodes (five half-hour programs) in one day, she works fourteen hours or more. She might be a little tired, but as soon as the cameras come on she impresses everyone by how completely professional she becomes.

And all the acting experience that she got in community theatre in Orlando paid off not long ago. She auditioned for a part in the movie "The Princess Diaries" and was named to be a part of the cast.

"It's a cool film," Mandy said, "and I get to play the really mean, crude, popular girl in the school who's always making out with her boyfriend. The one who gets ice cream in her face. It's going to be fun. I'm looking forward to it."

Julie Andrews is the star in the new film. She appeared in the movie version of "The Sound of Music." Mandy acted

At fifteen, she became one of the youngest hosts in MTV's history.

Mandy is getting her first break in the movies from powerhouse director Garry Marshall.

in "The Sound of Music" when she was doing community theatre in Orlando.

"The Princess Diaries" is directed by Garry Marshall, who knows something about movie stars. The creator of the 1970s hit TV show "Happy Days," he also directed "Pretty Woman" in 1990. That movie made Julia Roberts a star. Could "The Princess Diaries" do the same thing for Mandy Moore?

Chapter 5
Growing Up

If you think that Mandy is very busy, you're right. Because of all the different things she does, she hasn't been able to attend school since her freshman year. So she has a tutor to help her with school subjects.

Between her singing, her acting, and her time on MTV's "Mandy," she works very long days. Because of all the demands on her time, sometimes it gets hard to tell people that she needs time to take a break and get eight hours of sleep.

Now that she's reached the place she's always dreamed of, she tries not to

Mandy's career does not allow time for school. She is tutored each day, instead.

let those demanding days get to her. Instead of complaining, she focuses on the many talented people who would love to be doing what she's doing. She never takes her success for granted, because she knows that being famous and successful can go away very quickly.

So Mandy Moore keeps motivated by trying to focus on what she truly loves—music. "I really wanted people to enjoy

Mandy with her new CD, "I Wanna Be With You."

my music as much as I enjoyed making it and creating it and recording it and performing it," she said.

Mandy Moore has focused on her dream for years. Despite obstacles, she never gave up. That's part of why she is where she is today.

Looking to the future, Mandy sees her music changing. Although she's currently recording another CD, her biggest goal now is to write the words to some of the songs she sings. She says the songs would be about personal things that reflect her own experiences and how she looks at life.

On her web site, MandyMoore.com, she tells her fans, "I don't feel I've missed out on anything about growing up, because I feel so fortunate. There are so many kids who would love to be doing what I'm doing!"

Mandy plans on doing exactly what's she's doing now for quite a while. And that's great news for everyone who enjoys her singing and acting.

Mandy plans to continue singing and acting for many more years.

Chronology

- 1984, born April 10 in Nashua, New Hampshire.
- 1984, moves with her family from New Hampshire to Orlando, Florida.
- 1990, sees the musical "Oklahoma" and realizes she wants to be a singer.
- 1993, begins performing National Anthem at Orlando sporting events.
- 1998, signs record deal with Epic/550 Records.
- 1999, tours as opening act for the groups 'N Sync and The Backstreet Boys.
- 1999, releases first album, "So Real."
- 2000, includes two songs in the film "Centerstage."
- 2000, releases Special Edition album "I Wanna Be With You."
- 2000, signs three-year deal with MTV, stars in own program "Mandy."
- 2001, stars in film *The Princess Diaries*.

Index